W9-BFB-362

Smart Animals

OCTOPUSES

by Michele Spirn

Consultant: Bill Murphy
Marine Biologist, Cold Marine Gallery
New England Aquarium
Boston, MA

BEARPORT
PUBLISHING

New York, New York

Credits

Cover and title page, © Reuters/CORBIS; 4, © SeaPics.com; 5, © Shedd Aquarium; 6L, © SeaPics.com; 6R, © Jeffrey L. Rotman/CORBIS; 7, © Fred Bavendam/Minden Pictures; 8, © Jeffrey L. Rotman/CORBIS; 9, © SeaPics.com; 10, © SeaPics.com; 11, © Fred Bavendam/Minden Pictures; 12, © Darryl Torckler/Stone/Getty Images; 13, © SeaPics.com; 14, © SeaPics.com; 15, Dave Herring; 16, © SeaPics.com; 17, © Stephen Frink/CORBIS; 18, © Museum Victoria; 19T, © Fred Bavendam/Minden Pictures; 19B, © Roger Steene/imagequestmarine.com; 20, © SeaPics.com; 21, © Jeffrey L. Rotman/CORBIS; 22, © Seafriends Marine Conservation and Education Centre; 23, © AP Photo/Chris Gardner; 24T, Dave Herring; 24B, © Jeffrey L. Rotman/CORBIS; 25, © Edith Widder/BHOI; 26, © Northwind Picture Archives; 27, © SeaPics.com; 28, © Fred Bavendam/Minden Pictures; 29, © Reuters/CORBIS.

Publisher: Kenn Goin
Project Editor: Adam Siegel
Creative Director: Spencer Brinker
Original Design: Dawn Beard Creative

Library of Congress Cataloging-in-Publication Data

Spirn, Michele.
  Octopuses / by Michele Spirn ; consultant, Bill Murphy.
    p. cm. — (Smart animals)
  Includes bibliographical references and index.
  ISBN-13: 978-1-59716-250-0 (library binding)
  ISBN-10: 1-59716-250-7 (library binding)
  ISBN-13: 978-1-59716-278-4 (pbk.)
  ISBN-10: 1-59716-278-7 (pbk.)
  1. Octopuses—Juvenile literature. 2. Octopuses—Psychology—Juvenile literature.
3. Animal intelligence—Juvenile literature. I. Title. II. Series.

  QL430.3.O2S65 2007
  594'.56—dc22
                        2006009881

For more information, write to Bearport Publishing Company, Inc., 101 Fifth Avenue, Suite 6R, New York, New York 10003. Printed in the United States of America.

10 9 8 7 6 5 4 3 2 1

Contents

A Brainy Breakfast

It was breakfast time at the Shedd **Aquarium** in Chicago. Ernie Sawyer was getting ready to feed a giant Pacific octopus. Usually he just put the food in the animal's tank. Today, however, would be different.

▲ **A giant Pacific octopus in the wild**

Animals that don't have backbones, such as octopuses, clams, jellyfish, and worms, are called **invertebrates**. Octopuses are the smartest kind of invertebrate.

Ernie put two shrimp and two fish in a plastic jar. Then he screwed on the top. Would the large, red octopus find a way to get his breakfast?

The octopus gripped the jar with his powerful arms. In less than three minutes the lid was off. That morning, the octopus didn't just get a tasty treat. He also got a chance to show off his brainpower.

▲ **This is the octopus in Chicago right after he removed the lid from the plastic jar.**

Smart Eaters

Opening jars to get food is just one way that octopuses have shown they can solve problems. In the wild, octopuses eat clams. They use their strong arms to pull apart the shells to get the meat inside. Scientists who studied octopuses wanted to see what would happen if they wired some clam shells shut. Would the octopuses still find a way to open the clams?

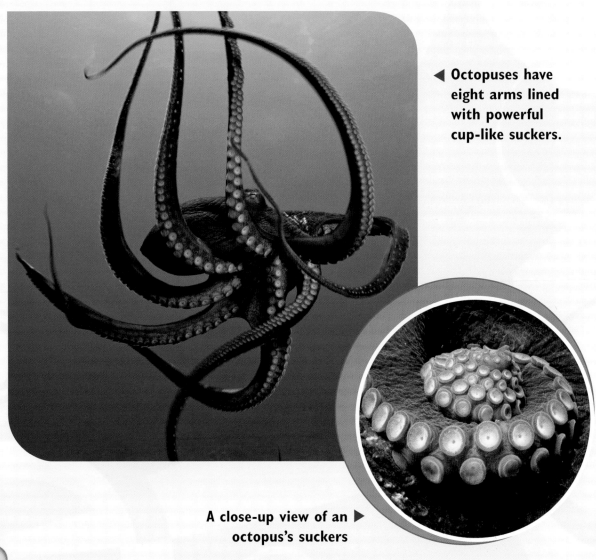

◀ Octopuses have eight arms lined with powerful cup-like suckers.

A close-up view of an ▶ octopus's suckers

The steel wire made it too hard for the octopuses to pull apart the shells with their arms. So they found another way to get the food inside. The octopuses used their parrot-like **beaks** to chip holes in the shells.

▲ **This octopus uses its suckers to hold two crabs it is going to eat. It will use its beak to break the crabs' shells to get the meat inside.**

Being able to solve problems is a sign of a smart animal.

Staying Safe

Octopuses have clever ways of getting food. Yet they have to be careful when hunting in the ocean. Octopuses don't have a hard outer shell, like snails and clams do, to protect themselves. They also don't have any bones. So their soft bodies make them an easy meal for sea animals, such as seals, sharks, and whales.

▲ **This dolphin is about to eat an octopus.**

To stay safe, octopuses need to find good places to hide from **predators**. Octopuses search for small cracks in rocks and **reefs**. Then they slide their bodies into the holes. They make their **lairs**, or homes, in the cracks. Octopuses stay in these lairs most of the time.

◄ **This octopus peeks out from a shell that it has squeezed into.**

Since an octopus has no bones, it can wiggle into a tiny space as long as there is room for its beak.

A Secret Weapon

Octopuses usually only leave their lairs at night to hunt for food. Yet other hungry predators may be **lurking** about at the same time. So octopuses need clever ways to escape from them. Luckily these animals have a secret weapon.

▲ **An octopus hunting for food at night**

If an octopus is under attack, it can squirt a cloud of black ink at its enemy. The ink darkens the water. It is now hard for the confused attacker to see the octopus. The cloudy water lets the eight-armed sea creature make a fast escape to safety.

▲ **An octopus squirting ink**

An octopus's ink cloud is sometimes shaped like its body, which can confuse the attacker even more.

Great Escapes

Sometimes an octopus changes its body color to black when it is shooting ink. Then the animal changes its color again, this time to white. The attacker chases the black cloud, thinking it is the octopus. In the meantime, the tricky white creature quickly returns back home.

▲ **An octopus squirting ink to get away from a diver**

Some **species** of octopuses may also fool an enemy by breaking off one of their own arms. While the predator eats the arm, the octopus makes a fast **exit**. In time, the octopus will grow a new arm.

An octopus's arm may keep moving after it is broken off. It may even crawl on an enemy.

◀ **A dragon moray eel can use its razor-sharp teeth to bite off an octopus's arm.**

Jetting Away

Most octopuses do not usually swim to get around. Instead, they use their arms to crawl along the ocean floor. When they are in danger, however, they can move quickly. How? They make their bodies act like jet engines. Instead of shooting out air to move, they use water!

When an octopus jets away, it travels headfirst with its long arms trailing behind.

First, the octopus sucks in water to fill the part of its body called the **mantle**. Then it uses its muscles to force the water out of its **siphon**, a tube-like body part. Water shoots out of the octopus, jetting it away to safety.

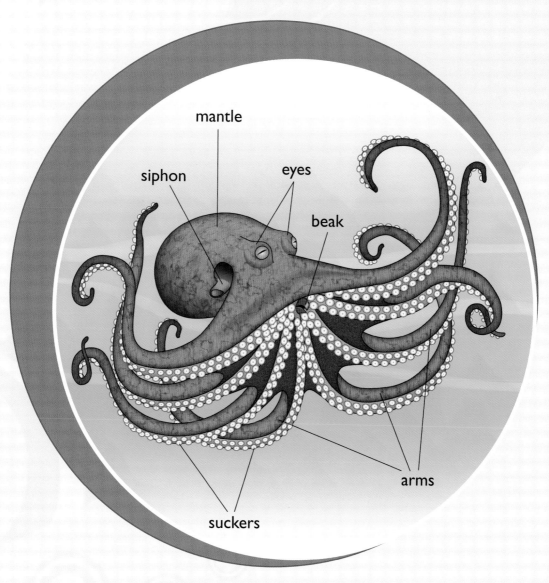

mantle

siphon   eyes

beak

arms

suckers

▲ **Parts of an octopus's body**

Masters of Disguise

Jetting away is important when an octopus is in danger. Often, however, predators can't see the **crafty** creature—even when it is right in front of them. Why? Octopuses are great at **disguising** themselves. In seconds they can change the color and **texture** of their bodies.

▲ This octopus matched the color of its body to the reef where it was resting.

An octopus's skin has thousands of tiny colored sacs that let the animal change its color. Its muscles can also make the skin look smooth or spiky. Put these abilities together and an octopus can easily hide from an enemy. It has no trouble blending in with a smooth, sandy ocean floor or a rocky reef.

◀ **An octopus that has blended in with its surroundings**

An octopus can change the way it looks 20 times in one minute.

Changing Shapes

The **mimic** octopus doesn't just blend in with its **environment**. It tricks enemies by making itself look like a dangerous sea creature.

▲ A mimic octopus

The mimic octopus was discovered in 1998. It can make itself look like many different creatures, including the **poisonous** lionfish.

For example, damselfish sometimes nip and bother mimic octopuses. Yet damselfish are afraid of banded sea snakes. So when the mimic octopus sees a damselfish, it hides six of its arms in the sand. It also changes its color to match the bands of the sea snake. When the damselfish sees the octopus's two arms sticking out, it gets afraid. It thinks it is seeing a sea snake and quickly swims away.

◄ A banded sea snake

◄ A mimic octopus pretending to be a banded sea snake

19

Taking Out the Trash

Scientists say that using **tools** is a sign of a smart animal. What kind of tool does an octopus use? It uses water, of course!

The pile of shells outside an octopus's lair is called a **midden**. Scientists look for middens to find out where octopuses live and what they eat.

◀ **Some people call a midden an "octopus's garden."**

Sometimes the hole where an octopus lives gets **clogged** with small rocks. So the octopus carries the **debris** to the front of its home. Then it uses its siphon to jet the rocks away with water. The octopus uses water to clean its home the way people use a broom to sweep away dirt.

Octopuses even clean up after meals. They use jets of water to push the empty shells out of their lairs. It's like taking out the trash.

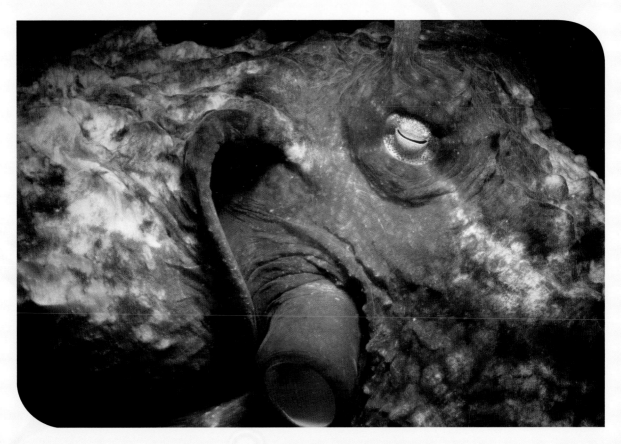

▲ **A close-up view of an octopus's siphon**

Playtime

Playing is also a sign of an intelligent animal. To test whether octopuses like to play, scientists at the Seattle Aquarium tossed an empty pill bottle into an octopus tank. The sea creatures squirted the bottle with water so that it circled around the tank. One octopus played for more than 20 minutes. Scientists said it was like a person bouncing a ball.

▲ A special program lets school children play with an octopus.

Other octopuses in tanks like to play with children's toys, such as plastic blocks and rubber animals. Some octopuses even like to play with people. They splash them with water or grab their hands with their arms.

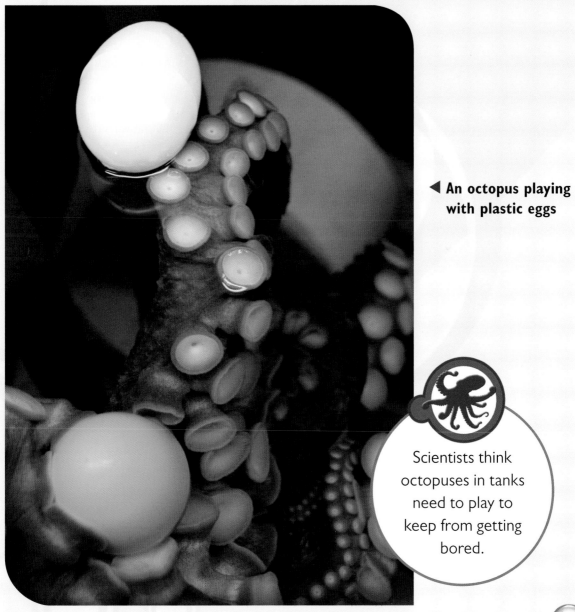

◄ **An octopus playing with plastic eggs**

Scientists think octopuses in tanks need to play to keep from getting bored.

Octopuses Everywhere

Octopuses live in oceans around the world. There are more than 250 different species. This map shows where the largest of these animals, the giant Pacific octopus, lives.

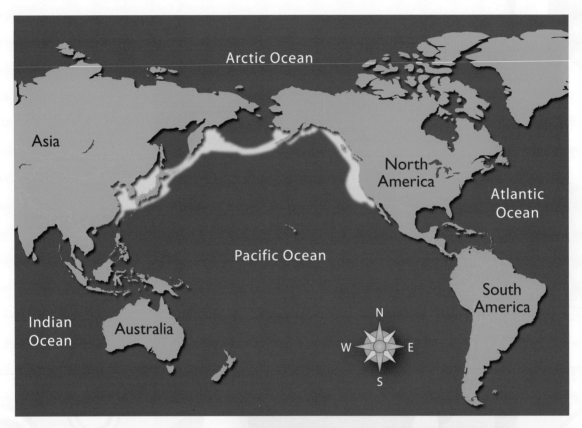

Arctic Ocean

Asia

North America

Atlantic Ocean

Pacific Ocean

Indian Ocean

Australia

South America

N
W E
S

■ Area where the giant Pacific octopus lives

Octopuses can live in strange places, or so it seems at first glance. One kind of octopus makes six of its arms look like a coconut shell. It uses the other two arms to walk along the ocean floor. When the "coconut" moves, predators don't even realize that they're looking at an octopus!

▲ **The suckers on this octopus can twinkle in the dark water.**

New kinds of octopuses are still being discovered. Recently, scientists found an octopus that has arms that glow in the dark.

Shy and Smart

Old sea stories often tell of deadly octopuses hiding at the bottom of the ocean. The evil creatures are waiting to crush ships and drag down sailors to their watery deaths. Scientists have learned, however, that octopuses don't really act this way.

▲ In movies and books, octopuses are wrongly shown as large monsters who wrap their arms around ships and people, crushing them to death.

Octopuses are shy and smart. They don't want to attack people. They want to be left alone. These intelligent animals can solve problems and use tools. They have clever ways of tricking enemies who want to turn them into a meal. Octopuses even like to play. These amazing sea creatures are not just unusual-looking, they are unusually bright.

▲ **Even the blue-ringed octopus, whose poisonous bite can kill people, tries to hide from humans. It usually only attacks when threatened.**

Some scientists think octopuses may be as smart as pet cats.

Just the Facts

Giant Pacific Octopus

Weight	about 50–90 pounds (23–41 kg); the largest one ever found was 600 pounds (272 kg)
Length	about 16 feet (5 m) from arm tip to arm tip
Life Span	3½–5 years
Habitat	rocky lairs in the Pacific Ocean from Alaska to Southern California, and around Japan and Korea
Food	shrimp, crabs, scallops, clams, and fish
Predators	harbor seals, sperm whales, and sea otters

More Smart Octopuses

One researcher made a puzzle where an octopus could get food by lifting a handle that raised a door. It took the scientist four hours to make the puzzle. The octopus solved the puzzle and found the food in 16 seconds.

By the time Frieda was about six months old, she had learned to use her arms to open a jar—but only if food was inside. She showed off her skills in Germany at Munich's Hellabrunn Zoo.

◀ Frieda is carrying a jar that holds her favorite snacks—shrimp, crabs, and clams.

Glossary

aquarium (uh-KWAIR-ee-uhm) a building where people can see different kinds of sea creatures

beaks (BEEKS) the hard, sharp parts of octopuses' mouths

clogged (KLOGD) blocked

crafty (KRAF-tee) clever

debris (duh-BREE) broken pieces of something

disguising (diss-GIZE-ing) looking like something else

environment (en-VYE-ruhn-muhnt) the plants, animals, and weather in a place

exit (EG-zit) the act of going away

invertebrates (in-VUR-tuh-brits) animals that don't have a backbone

lairs (LAIRZ) the homes of wild animals, such as octopuses

lurking (LURK-ing) secretly hiding

mantle (MAN-tuhl) the muscular covering that surrounds the main body of an octopus

midden (MID-uhn) a pile of shells that an octopus has left outside its lair

mimic (MIM-ik) to copy

poisonous (POI-zuhn-uhss) able to kill or harm someone

predators (PRED-uh-turz) animals that hunt other animals for food

reefs (REEFS) chains of rocks or coral near the water's surface

siphon (SYE-fuhn) a tube-shaped part of an octopus's body that is used to let out water

species (SPEE-sheez) groups that animals are divided into, according to similar characteristics; members of the same species can have offspring together

texture (TEKS-chur) the way something looks and feels

tools (TOOLZ) equipment that is used to do a job

Bibliography

Blaxland, Beth. *Cephalopods: Octopuses, Squids, and Their Relatives.* Philadelphia: Chelsea House Publishers (2002).

Hirschi, Ron. *Octopuses.* Minneapolis, MN: Carolrhoda Books, Inc. (2000).

Read More

Cerullo, Mary. *The Octopus: Phantom of the Sea.* New York: Dutton Children's Books (1997).

Rhodes, Mary Jo, and David Hall. *Octopuses and Squids (Undersea Encounters).* Danbury, CT: Children's Press (2005).

Stille, Darlene. *Octopuses.* Chicago: Heinemann Library (2003).

Learn More Online

Visit these Web sites to learn more about octopuses:

www.ngeo.com/ngkids/0410/index.html

www.pbs.org/wnet/nature/octopus

www.royalbcmuseum.bc.ca/programs/expert/octopus

Index

About the Author

Michele Spirn has written more than 60 fiction and nonfiction books for children, including books on roller coasters, escalators, crocodiles, snakes, frogs, and unusual places and people.